A Celebration Of Angels

Inspired Writings
By
Sandra J Yearman

Seraphim Publishing LLC

WE WILL BRING LIGHT TO ALL THE DARK PLACES

Registered trademark-Sandra J Yearman
Seraphim Publishing
438 Water St
Cambridge, WI 53523

Copyright © 2008 Sandra J Yearman
Produced in the United States of America
Author : Sandra J Yearman
Editor: Sandra J Yearman
Cover Design by Sandra J Yearman
Layout and design by Sandra J Yearman

All rights reserved. No part of this book may be reproduced, stored in or introduced into a retrieval system, or transmitted, in any form or by any means, electronic or mechanical, including photocopying or recording or otherwise copied for public or private use—other than for "fair use" as brief quotations embodied in articles and reviews-without written permission from the author.

Library of Congress Control Number: 2009901985
ISBN: 978-0-9815791-3-9
First Edition

Blessed Be All
Who Sing The
Song Of God
For The Holy Spirit
Will Carry Them Home
Amen
Amen
Amen

CONTENTS

DEDICATION

A Celebration Of Angels..7
Truth Rings..10
I AM The Source..12
Inspiration..16
Disciples...17
Battle After Battle..19
Invisible Friends..21
Walked Upon This Earth.......................................23
Salvation..25

SEEKING LIGHT IN THE DARKNESS

In the Wilderness..27
To Whom Do We Pray..30
Behind The Masks...33
The Passions..35
When Man Calls To Darkness...............................37
Life...39
The Tears Of Angels..41
The Flock...43
Lord I Pray Today..45
Destruction Without Reason..................................46

CONTENTS

God Walk With Our Troops..............................48
Demons In The Garden.....................................50
The Past..52
I Spoke With A Soldier..55
Life Be Given...57
To Stay...59

COMING HOME

The Awakening..61
Mystical Journey...62
Sonship..64
Remembering The Face Of God.........................66
God In All His Mercy...68
Missions..70
Twilight In The Night Sky..................................73
Harmony..75
Dance In Radiant Love.......................................79

Dedication

A Celebration Of Angels

Your children gather here for worship
God You are the Song our hearts sing
Our voices raised in praise most Holy
Bless us with the Fire the Holy Spirit brings

One voice we raise to Heaven
Lord, Redeemer, Holy One
God the Song, God the Savior
Father, Spirit, Blessed Son

The Holy Spirit is in this place
God has filled us with His Grace
Our thanks we will always sing
To Jesus Christ our Heavenly King

In this place we will fill our cups with
Holiness
Our lips will taste the wine
Our hearts will be healed forever
The Fire of the Lord will be our sign

God touch all who enter here
Let this place be Your Home
Consume us with Your Presence
With You we are never alone

The Holy Spirit is in this place
God has filled us with His Grace
Our thanks we will always sing
To Jesus Christ our Heavenly King

This place is filled with Holiness
With Heaven we will commune
We surrender all to the Source
The Cross will always consume

Across these plains of existence
Will our voices ring
We will join the ranks of Heaven
With the Angels we will sing

Amen Amen Amen

Truth Rings

He came in the vessel of humanity
And wore the Crown of a King
The Angels sang in Heaven
As Holiness did ring

The altars of the Ancients
Ringed with a golden glow
As the Word of God was sent
To the dying worlds below

The ones who searched for Heaven
With faith and piety
Recognized their Savior
The Holy One in Three

Truth rings through the ages
For all who search and seek
The Word still dwells among us
The pious and the meek

He came in the vessel of humanity
And wore the Crown of a King
The Angels sang in Heaven
As Holiness did ring

Amen Amen Amen

I AM The Source

The God of your fathers
Heard My cries
I stand before creation
He will not let you die

I AM the Son
I AM the Source
I was sent to save
To teach the Course

To show you the Way to your Father
The path through the Son
The Redemption of man
The Unblemished One

The God of your fathers
Heard My cries
I stand before creation
He will not let you die

The gifts that I gave
The blessings I brought
Communion with Heaven
A blessing I taught

That you can speak with the Father
Pray to the Son
Praise the Holy Spirit
The Holy Three in One

Without intermediaries
Without riches and gold
Your Father is Love
A message of old

Communion with Heaven
Ask to bring the Spirit into your heart
Pray for forgiveness
That Holy Light may be a part

Of your daily existence
Of your thoughts and your prayers
Of your motivations
To heal your worries and cares

The God of your fathers
Heard My cries
I stand before creation
He will not let you die

I AM the Son
I AM the Source
I was sent to save
To teach the Course

Amen Amen Amen

Inspiration

Inspiration
The touching of souls

The worlds
Transcend

The boundaries
Unite

The Face of God
On this world shines bright

When He whispers
The souls sing with Grace

And God's inspiration
Is brought to this place

Amen Amen Amen

Disciples

A man walked with God
All the world did tell
That God had sent His Son
To save us all from hell

The Comforter was with them
The disciples He made strong
To Inspire and to teach them
To save a world gone wrong

They were anointed
By Spirit were they led
To heal a dying world
To tell of Him who had been raised
from the dead

He gave them their own voices
Yet they spoke with many tongues
To bring Light into the darkness
To sing of the Blessed One

Miracles God created
Through these brave and Holy men
To remind God's children
How to find the path to Heaven, to remind them to ascend

Amen Amen Amen

Battle After Battle

An Angel came from Heaven
To answer the dying call
Of soldiers, children in battle
Who had given their very all

Brave were the warriors
Heavy were their souls
For the weight of sin and battle
Takes a worldly toll

Families that were broken
Children yet unborn
For the fallen soldiers
A waiting world does mourn

Battle after battle
Darkness is the test
The Angel showed us God's Light
That darkness, we may surpass

God in all His Glory
Created this precious life
He sent His Son as the Answer
To escape the hell and strife

Amen Amen Amen

Invisible Friends

The wings of Angels flutter
As the children's voices sound
The prayers of the babes
Summoning Angels to surround

The voices in their innocence
Are gifts that God holds dear
When the voices of the children
Call the Hosts of Heaven near

They are our ever companions
They are our friends in Right
The wings of Angels flutter
As they protect us in the night

The child sees through illusions
Sees the invisible friends
As the wings of Angels flutter
In a world that has no end

Amen Amen Amen

Walked Upon This Earth

An Angel came from Heaven
And walked upon this earth
She filled the winds with love
Compassion and Holy mirth

She protected those she loved
With honor beyond belief
She cried the tears of Heaven
And healed a world of grief

She fought a dangerous demon
And lost a friend as well
She conquered all the darkness
And saved that friend from hell

She danced in a garden
She blew life into the dead
She made promises to God
And accomplished all she said

When her missions ended
She cried with great relief
For the Light she brought from Heaven
Grew into a great Fire of belief

Amen Amen Amen

Salvation

Darkness has no thunder
Darkness has no hold
The Father sent the Son
Salvation as fore told

The darkness shrieks with horror
As the Son rises in the skies
And saves the children of the Lord
The blessed and the wise

In the darkest caverns
In the storm tossed seas
The Light of Heaven will prevail
Salvation for you and me

Horror has its boundaries
Only the Lord is without end
Eternal is His Presence
Amen, Amen, Amen

Seeking Light In The Darkness

In The Wilderness

'Sons of My children'
'Call out My Name'
'The answers that you seek'
'The Truths are the same'

Wandering in the wilderness
Looking for a Home
We are lost in the nightmares
Anchored in darkness we roam

We fill our lives with turmoil
We fail to seek the Truth
We build demons out of gold
Is humanity but a ruse

'Sons of My children'
'Call out My Name'
'The answers that you seek'
'The Truths are the same'

Ask forgiveness for your actions
Ask guidance for your fears
Seek the Face of Heaven
The Angels will draw near

Rebuke not the Father
Believe in the Son
Conquer the obstacles
A race that is run

'Sons of My children'
'Call out My Name'
'The answers that you seek'
'The Truths are the same'

Amen Amen Amen

To Whom Do We Pray

An Angel showed me an image
Of darkness as we are told
In the vessel of a creature
Who worships pain and gold

As I watched this creature
It grew before my eyes
Until it spread its darkness
Through the human skies

I asked the Angel
'What are you showing me'
He said, 'This is the world of man'
'When children do not call upon the
Holy One in Three'

I saw that the darkness
Takes on many forms
I saw it walk among
I heard it sing our songs

I saw people adorn it
And pray upon their knees
I asked the Angel
'Why aren't they praying to the Holy
One in Three'

He slowly answered
I saw a tear upon his face
'The children get lost'
'In the darkness of this place'

'They call out to the darkness'
'The choice is always theirs'
'They hide from the fact'
'That they are God's Holy Heirs'

'But for those who honesty call God's Name'
'God will send His Angels to stand before them'
'And bring them Home'
To their Holy inheritance in Heaven'

Amen Amen Amen

Behind The Masks

The world stood in wonder
As darkness took control
People too afraid
To save their very souls

Children lost to horror
Mothers devoured sons
Humans lost conception
From where they had begun

Fathers selling children
Children trained to hate
When darkness rules our world
What is humanity's fate

Demons hide their faces
Afraid the Son will see
Because darkness is not as strong
As the Holy One in Three

Amen Amen Amen

The Passions

Angels see forever
God in Holy Grace
The Heavens are Eternal
Children seek God's Holy Face

Heaven is a life force
That sees all that we do
That hears the cries to Heaven
That knows what we must undo

Only Heaven knows
The fears and motivations
The crimes and the deeds
The prayers and tribulations

The wants and the needs
The deepest desires
The dreams that we long
The passions and the fires

Amen Amen Amen

When Man Calls To Darkness

The child asked her grandfather
'What do these numbers mean'
'They were stamped by a demon'
He cried, 'Not a human being'

'There was a time when the demons'
'Almost took control'
'Every man, woman and child'
'Were endanger of losing their souls'

'Demons walked among us'
'More than there are now'
'And when the dust had settled'
'The entire world asked, "How"

'Could we have let that happen'
'Let fear and hatred take control'
'How could we let a few'
'Terrorize so many souls'

The demon marks his victims
Although the numbers are not always seen
When man calls to darkness
And offers up his being

Amen Amen Amen

Life

I have seen horror
Its face will stay with me all my days
The test is not to let its darkness conquer
Not to sink, not to decay

Death can wear many faces
The demons do as well
The challenge is to conquer
And not to exist where they dwell

God tests us always
This life may be a battle ground
The choices that we make
In Heaven do resound

God I will pray to Heaven
To God, One in Three
To take this journey with me
To take a walk with Thee

Amen Amen Amen

The Tears Of Angels

The tears of Angels
Are shed this night
For the condition of men
Their fears and their plight

If only God's children
Would call out His Name
To protect and to shelter
To cleanse them from shame

Altars abandoned
Faith not restored
Calling to darkness
Mankind abhor

When did we lose sight
When did we cease
To desire the Light
Instead of darkness increase

God in Your Mercy
God in Your Love
Fill us with Your Heavenly
Light from above

The tears of Angels
Are shed this night
For the condition of men
Their fears and their plight

Amen Amen Amen

The Flock

The flock calls to Holy men
To help them seek God's Face
But their darkness permeates
Instead they fall from Grace

They hide behind words and guise
They claim to know God's Ways
Who really wears their masks
Instead they fall from Grace

Seek the Path and seek the Truth
Conquer the barriers we create
Ask for God to Consume you
Ask to be filled with Holy Grace

Nothing hides from Heaven
No one escapes God's eye
Heaven knows all motivations
God sees through every guise

The Holy men were wounded
The Holy men were killed
By those who boasted they knew God's
Ways
By those who claimed they knew
God's Will

The Pharisees among us
Exist in every race
Every culture, every time
They exist in every place

Amen Amen Amen

Lord I Pray Today

Lord I pray today
For all the littered bodies
For all those who die alone

Whose existence passes
And no one notices
And no one cares

Lord I shed a tear
For even the smallest of creation
No life is so insignificant

That it should die alone
Unloved
Unnoticed

Amen Amen Amen

Destruction Without Reason

Has man declared war on creation
To fill the darkest need
Unbridled devastation
To the Holy signs, they do not heed

Murder through the ages
Hatred without end
Will they ever listen
To the messages that God sends

Destroy all that sustains us
Plunder what remains
Humiliate nature
The actions of the insane

Destruction without reason
A course that man has laid
What motivates our actions
What covenants are made

God save us from our darkness
Bless the life You created
Help us to see the Holy signs
Before all life is annihilated

Amen Amen Amen

God Walk With Our Troops

May the wings of Angels
Shelter our troops tonight
God watch over them
Protect them in their plight

Heal their wounds
The fear and the pain
Comfort them in sadness
Your Glory to gain

Shower them with Mercy
Cleanse them with Light
Protect them with Love
From the demons in the night

Lift them above
The insanity of man
God walk with our troops
God take a Holy stand

They are Your children
The warriors in the night
Bless and protect them
Keep them in Your Holy Sight

Amen Amen Amen

Demons In The Garden

God created a garden
That no man's eyes could behold
For silver and for riches
Man, the garden sold

God filled the garden with blessings
He sent His Angels in
To teach of His Love
But His children chose to sin

They could not face their actions
Or the consequences of their sins
They justified their darkness
By saying 'God would not let them in'

They allowed demons to desecrate the
Holiest
Of places and of things
They justified their darkness
By saying 'God would not let them in'

They put the shackles on themselves
They chose the lives of sin
They justified their darkness
By saying 'God would not let them in'

Amen Amen Amen

The Past

Years of pain and worry
Showed upon his face
Everyday was lifeless
Because of the misery of his place

Daily he went to the remnants
Of an old remembered place
He prayed and screamed to Heaven
For the curse upon his face

As he remained in the shell of his memories
Crying because he had been wronged
A child came upon him
A child who lived God's Song

She asked him why he cried
Why he chose to stay in this place
Where the clouds had been called to hide
The Holiness of God's Grace

He cried out that 'God had left him'
He said he 'Was waiting to go Home'
The child Angel blessed him
'God is here, it is you who chose to roam'

'God has never left you'
'You chose darkness, which was wrong'
'And every time He speaks to you'
'You block out the sweetness of His Song'

'He sends you many messages'
'He sends you many signs'
'You choose not to listen'
'You make your eyes blind'

'God sends His Angels'
'Into this world of man'
'To protect you and to guide you'
'To take you by the hand'

'But you have been blessed'
'With the freedom to choose it all'
'To let God in; to take the hand He sends you'
'No matter how small'

Amen Amen Amen

I Spoke With A Soldier

I spoke with a soldier yesterday
Eyes that would reveal
The trauma of a soul
The wounds that would not heal

The wind blows sand forever
The children that are lost
Wars throughout the ages
Conflicts at what cost

Child-men in the darkness
Turmoil without end
Bodies that are tortured
Spirits that can not transcend

I spoke with a soldier yesterday
Eyes that would tell
Of a soul that was dwindling
Of a man exposed to hell

God bless our soldiers
Keep them in Your care
Blow life back into their beings
Their yokes, more than they can bear

God shield them with Your Presence
Protect them with Your Might
Heal the wounds that kill
The wounds that keep them in the night

Amen Amen Amen

Life Be Given

This
I do not understand
The insanity
Of the world of man

Life
Yet they crave
All their choices
Lead to the grave

Gifts
Sent from Heaven
They choose fear
Their lives are driven

Light
They claim to seek
But it is to the darkness
That they speak

Illusions
They create
The maze increases
They are blind to the Gate

Son
Sent from Heaven
To deliver them
And Life be given

Amen Amen Amen

To Stay

A monster they created
A monster that they wed
They created the illusions
They gave it form, they said

Did we contain the monster
When life began that day
Or is it just man's calling
That makes the darkness stay

We created the fear
From which we can not run away
Unless we surrender to the Lord
And ask the Holy Spirit to stay

Amen Amen Amen

Coming Home

The Awakening

A breath
A Star
A shadow walking

An illusion
A Voice
Stillness talking

A dove
An eagle
Angels calling

The Breath o f Life
Illusions falling

Amen Amen Amen

Mystical Journey

Floating in the abyss
Disconnecting from all around
Belonging to neither world
Disassociated with what grounds

Journey through the darkness
Individuals instead of the mass
Drifting through the illusions
Searching behind the masks

Searching for the meanings
Traveling through time and space
Letting go of attachments
In the God forsaken place

A journey to remember
The veils to uplift
Follow the Light through the darkness
The mystic finds the gift

Amen Amen Amen

Sonship

I saw the Face of God tonight
In the eyes of one I hold dear
This revelation let me know
That God is always near

I know that He surrounds me
I feel His Presence here
Because I call out to the Heavens
To bring His Spirit near

I see the Face of Heaven
In the dawn, as it was meant
I hear His Song in nature
We are blessed by what He has sent

And every time a flower grows
I hear a Voice that speaks
'If you believe in His Love and in His Life'
'You'll find the Face you seek'

Amen Amen Amen

Remembering The Face Of God

I tried to paint a picture
Of God as I was told
Of the image of a man
Of Holiness to behold

But how do you paint an image
Of vastness beyond belief
Of Beauty and of Spirit
When man can barely see past his human grief

How do you put Love on canvas
How is Holiness shown
To paint Faith is more than an art
How do we comprehend the unknown

How do you define existence
That is beyond our time and space
When we are self absorbed and
 confused
And can not see past our own race

As I pondered the Face of God
A tribute I would create
To my God and to my Father
The Son who is the Holy Gate

I realized I could not paint Him
With the limits of my mind
So I painted the canvas in whites and
gold
For illumination was my sign

Amen Amen Amen

God In All His Mercy

Angels walk among us
Birds will sing on high
God in all His Mercy
Saved us from the night

Angels will rescue the victims
Angels will sing on high
God in all His Mercy
His Justice restores the right

Angels stand before us
God sends His messengers
As protectors, guides and teachers
As prophets and harbingers

God in all His Mercy
Love and Comforter
Saves the lost and lonely
Saves the unheard

God will not forsake you
He will not leave in your pain
Call upon Him
All Holiness to gain

Amen Amen Amen

Missions

She cried out to the Heavens
To be consumed with God's Song
So she could remember Heaven
Her Home where she belonged

The Angels sang with sweetness
The Angels taught the words
The Heavenly melody filled her
The Holy energy surged

An Angel sent from Heaven
To protect the children here
Her mission was most Holy
The Heavens she called near

She cried the tears of Heaven
Compassion filled her heart
For the victims and the weak
The forgotten and the dark

A warrior in her birth right
An Angel in her soul
The wisdom of the ages
To teach Holiness was her goal

She wrote the words of Heaven
She sang the Holy Songs
She brought Light into the darkness
She saved them from their wrongs

The Angels sang with sweetness
The Angels taught the words
The Heavenly melody filled her
The Holy energy surged

God in all His Mercy
God with all His Might
Will always send us Miracles
To escape the darkness of the night

Amen Amen Amen

Twilight In The Night Sky

Twilight in the night sky
Stars that would behold
Images walk among us
Miracles be told

Light that draws life to it
Light that shows the Way
Light that warms the conscience
Light of each new day

Worlds that whirl around us
Mysteries be told
Angels dance to music
The Song that saves the souls

God change our eyes to see You
Our hearts to hear Your Voice
Awaken the mystery within us
This our Holy Choice

Amen Amen Amen

Harmony

I had a Holy vision
The splendor will always remain with me
The Angel that I saw
Was filled with Love and Harmony

I was crying in the darkness
My head was in my hands
When the room was filled with brightness
And my legs could no longer stand

The image that I witnessed
Was beauty to behold
I saw a Holy Angel
With long hair of flaxen gold

On her shoulder was an eagle
A lion at her side
Three tigers walked behind her
I thought that I had died

As I looked with wonder
I saw more of life appear
Images of creation
The Angel told me not to fear

I was filled with warmth
Love replaced my fright
I was no longer seeing
The images of the night

I saw beasts of every nature
And humans of every race
I saw trees and waterfalls
This image was a wonderful place

I cried out to the Angel
'I do not understand'
'This image that you show me'
'Is this the world of man'

I heard a voice like music
'You pray for all the nations, for creatures you hold dear'
'You cry out for salvation, for a decaying world'
'That is filled with hatred and fear'

The Angel went on saying
'You call upon God's Grace'
'You have overcome the challenges'
'You have won the arduous race'

'And all that God holds scared'
'His children of every creed'
'The humans, plants and animals'
'In your world, are in dire need'

God celebrates His children
Who understand the Holy tapestry
The missions and the challenges
The Love of One in Three

Amen Amen Amen

Dance In Radiant Love

Bless God and all of Heaven
For the Blessings that You brought
For the Love and Understanding
For the Message we have sought

Bless God the Holy Father
The Spirit Three In One
Who saved a dying world
Through the Blessings of the Son

Bless the Holy Angels
Who tend us as their sheep
Who guide us and protect us
The covenants to keep

Bless the Holy Lamb Jesus
Who died that we may live
Who brought us God's Blessings
A symbol of the Love that God gives

Let the Hosts of Heaven
Dance in radiant Love
A celebration of Angels
To the Glory of God, above

Amen Amen Amen

And We Will Dance
To Heavenly Music
Amen
Amen
Amen

www.ingramcontent.com/pod-product-compliance
Lightning Source LLC
Chambersburg PA
CBHW051711040426
42446CB00008B/832